THE GIVING TREES NEED YOUR HELP!

TREES FOR KIDS

Biology 3rd Grade
Children's Biology Books

BABY PROFESSOR

EDUCATION KIDS

Speedy Publishing LLC

40 E. Main St. #1156

Newark, DE 19711

www.speedypublishing.com

Copyright 2017

In this book, we're going to cover the importance of trees and how you can help forests stay healthy. So, let's get right to it!

Air Pollution

WHY ARE TREES DYING WORLDWIDE?

Greenhouse gases, especially carbon dioxide, caused by car emissions and industrial processes are trapping heat in the atmosphere. This heat is changing our climate on Earth. Trees are dying worldwide in record numbers. Because they can't move, trees are vulnerable to the shifts in temperatures caused by global warming. It's estimated that about 5 billion trees are being lost globally every year.

Intense climate events such as droughts and extreme heat are causing trees to die out entire forests at a time. The remaining trees are weakened and become susceptible to insect pests as well as disease. In addition to the indirect way that humans are causing tree destruction, we're also causing it by chopping down trees and rainforests without replacing them.

Drought

Trees

WHY ARE TREES SO IMPORTANT?

Trees are vital to life on Earth. They provide oxygen, shelter, and food. Without trees, not much if any life would survive on Earth. They cover almost one third of the Earth's land today, but their numbers are decreasing.

TREES GIVE OXYGEN

Trees take in the carbon dioxide we exhale when we breathe and release life-giving oxygen, which people, animals, and plants need to survive. The problem is that the amount of carbon dioxide being spewed into the atmosphere is excessive and is causing the Earth's temperature to change.

J ust one leafy tree can give as much oxygen in one season as ten people need for an entire year. Trees account for about 30% of the oxygen we and other animals breathe.

Squirrel

TREES SHELTER ANIMALS

Half of the known species worldwide make forests their home. There are at least seven different types of forests throughout the world.

Every type of forest is home to different types of animals. For example, tropical rainforests are home to exotic birds and apes while deer, raccoons, and porcupines live in temperate forests.

TREES SHELTER PEOPLE

Worldwide, over 300 million people dwell in the forest and one-fifth of them are native people who depend on the forest for their day-to-day survival. In urban areas, trees make a difference too. They provide beauty, raise property values, and make the environment pleasing, which actually reduces crime.

Korowai house on a tree

Boreal Forest

TREES KEEP US COOL

Trees divert sunlight and create shade, helping houses and urban buildings stay cool. Large forests help to regulate temperatures and assist in curbing the heat effect of cities. They help keep the Earth cool too.

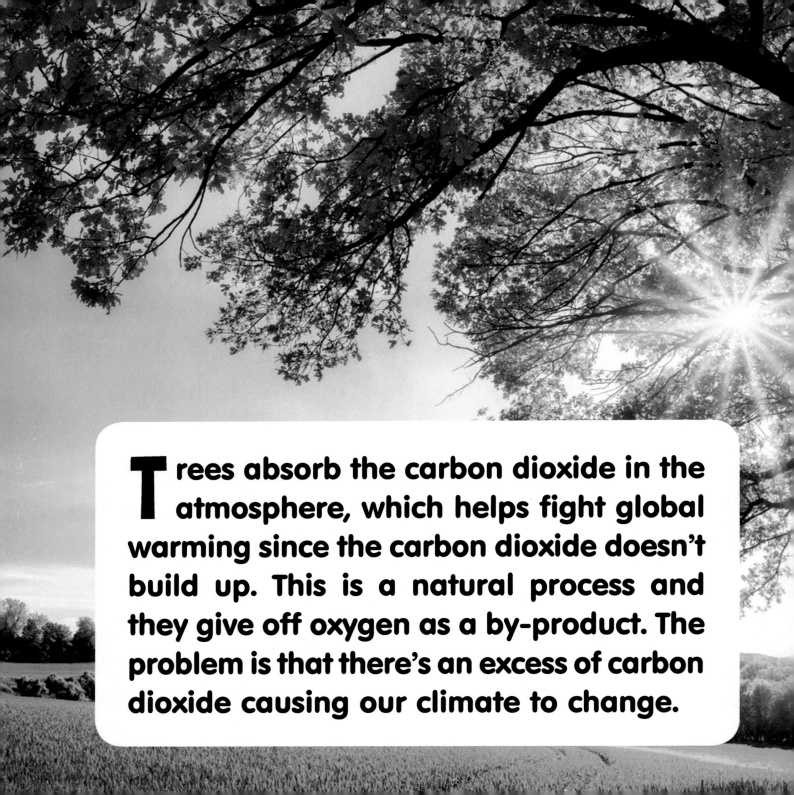

Trees absorb the carbon dioxide in the atmosphere, which helps fight global warming since the carbon dioxide doesn't build up. This is a natural process and they give off oxygen as a by-product. The problem is that there's an excess of carbon dioxide causing our climate to change.

Rainforest

TREES INFLUENCE RAIN

In addition to helping to cool off temperatures, trees influence weather patterns and can even develop their own microclimates. For example, the influence of the Amazon rainforest in Brazil extends over a wide area. It promotes rainfall in its location as well as farmlands that are located nearby, but it also influences weather as far away as North America.

TREES FIGHT FLOODING

When there are heavy rains, trees prevent low-lying areas such as river plains from getting flooded. They soak up the water in their roots preventing the ground from getting overly saturated. They minimize the loss of valuable soil and help prevent property damage by reducing the water's flow.

Flooded community

By soaking up surface runoff, they protect downstream ecosystems from toxins, fertilizers, and pesticides. They take the brunt of these toxins, and in doing so prevent other environments from getting toxic.

They don't soak up all the water, but by slowing the water down the trickle off goes down into aquifers, the underground rocks that transmit water. This replenishes the groundwater that is used in irrigation, sanitation, and for drinking.

TREES BLOCK EXCESS WIND

Farmers who plant their crops near a forest gain benefits. The trees break the wind so that it doesn't damage sensitive plants. It's easier for bees to pollinate the crops when there is less wind too. Songbirds and bats from the forest eat up pest insects and woodland owls and foxes keep the rats in check.

TREES KEEP SOIL IN PLACE

The complex root system of a forest braces the soil against the attacks of wind and water. When a forest is cut down, there's nothing to prevent soil erosion. The resulting loose soil sometimes triggers deadly landslides and dust storms.

Trees also help clean up the toxins in soil from sewage or toxic spills.

TREES HELP CLEAN DIRTY AIR

Just like houseplants help purify air inside your house, forests help clean up air pollution on a larger scale. They soak up chemicals like nitrogen dioxide, sulfur dioxide, and carbon monoxide. They can't completely eliminate air pollution but they help to reduce it.

coconut tree

TREES FEED US AND OTHER ANIMALS

Trees provide us with edible fruits, seeds, nuts, and even sap that we use for syrup. Birds eat their berries, squirrels eat their nuts, and insects eat their sap.

TREES HELP US CONSTRUCT THINGS

Timber and resin from trees have helped us make paper, clothing, furniture, and even the homes we live in for thousands of years. Unfortunately, our human needs have sometimes meant overuse. Today, many governments and organizations understand the need for keeping our forests safe. Tree farming and safer, more sustainable practices in forestry have led to tree products that are sourced more responsibly.

Lumber

Noni Fruit

Used for treating abdominal pains

TREES GIVE US VALUABLE MEDICINES

Trees provide natural medicines. For example, the drug theophylline used to fight asthma comes from the cacao tree. About 70 percent of cancer-fighting plants grow only in rainforests.

TREES CREATE JOBS

More than 1.5 billion people depend on forests to earn a living. Forest management as well as conservation employs over 10 million people. Many developing countries are dependent on the commerce from non-timber products.

Fruit pickers

A wide park path with blooming cherry trees

TREES PROVIDE NATURAL BEAUTY

If you've ever walked under a canopy of rustling leaves, you know how beautiful and restful being around trees can be. They provide a feeling of connection to the Earth and all of nature.

WHAT CAN YOU DO TO HELP TREES?

Environmental groups, governments, and communities are working hard to help trees by preventing deforestation and keeping toxic carbon dioxide emissions to a minimum. You can do things to help trees too. Everything helps!

Tree Planting

Recycled paper origami

CUT DOWN ON USING PAPER

When you need paper, buy recycled paper. By using less paper, you'll prevent trees from being cut down. Get into the habit of reusing paper. Use a box to keep paper that's only used on one side. Then you can use the other side for homework or a grocery list. If your school allows you to submit your homework online, then you won't need paper at all!

Use cloth napkins instead of paper ones and cloth hand towels instead of paper towels. Instead of using a paper bag for your lunch, get a reusable lunchbox that you can wash every day and reuse.

Recycled paper wallet

REDUCE, RECYCLE AND REUSE WHENEVER POSSIBLE

Once you're done with paper and can't use it anymore, make sure to recycle it. You can also recycle glass and plastic containers. Recycling helps to decrease the greenhouse gases that come from landfills. Most communities offer recycling services now so you can put out your recycling once a week.

PLANT TREES

You can plant trees on Earth Day in April and you can also beautify your yard and other community spaces by planting trees in the fall, when it's tree-planting season.

STAY ON TRAILS

There's a reason that when you visit the forest, signs say to "stay on trails." Those signs are for your own safety, but they're also for another reason. If you stay on the trails, you minimize human impact on wilderness areas so they'll stay preserved for the future.

DON'T START FIRES

Fires started by humans are still a huge hazard for forests. No matter where you are, don't play with matches or lighters. If camping outdoors, be careful with fire and make sure your campfire is out before you leave it unattended.

Lightning and lava can start forest fires, but about 90% of the fires in the United States are caused by people who leave campfires unattended, throw cigarettes on the ground or burn debris without the proper precautions. Some criminals set fires deliberately too.

YOUR PARENTS CAN HELP TOO

If you have a new baby at your house, your mom can use cloth diapers instead of disposable ones. Disposable diapers have to go to landfills after they're used.

At the grocery store, use reusable canvas bags instead of using plastic or paper bags that have to be thrown away.

You can do your part to help trees survive on Earth so they can keep giving oxygen, shelter, food, and beauty to us.

Canvas Grocery Bag

Awesome! Now you know some simple things you can do to help conserve trees. You can find more books about Biology from Baby Professor by searching the website of your favorite book retailer.

Made in the USA
Las Vegas, NV
24 January 2023

66183337R00040